How to

Enjoy Reading Aloud

to young children

Edmund Pegge & Alison Shakspeare

SOUTHGATE

• PUBLISHERS •

Copyright text © Edmund Pegge and Alison Shakspeare 2007
First published 2007 by Southgate Publishers Ltd
Reprinted 2008 twice

Southgate Publishers Ltd, The Square, Sandford, Crediton, Devon EX17 4LW

Printed and bound in Great Brirain by HSW Print, Tonypandy, Rhondda, Wales.

British Library Cataloguing in Publication Data
A CIP catalogue record for this book is available from the British Library.

ISBN 1–85741–156–0   ISBN 9781857411560

Acknowledgements
Designed by Chris Wakefield.
Thanks to the following for their expert help and advice:
Ali Perry, Voluntary Action Kennet
Clare Eastland
Mary Ritson and Jacky Brennan, Bluecoat Children's Centre.

Contents

Good things about
reading aloud

This book concentrates on HOW to read aloud with tips and fun ideas to boost your confidence and ability.

Reading aloud really is one of the most important things you can do with your child to help them succeed in life because:

- it increases their confidence with words
- it develops their understanding of the world
- It improves their listening skills
- it is a fun way to develop your relationship.

There is lots more advice and help on offer about **why** you should read aloud, and what books you could use. If you want to find out more about all that then look at the last page.

Comfort tips

The more relaxed you are the more fun you will have so:

- choose a book you enjoy – it'll make it easier
- get comfortable and cosy – but not so you'll fall asleep!
- gently encourage your child to join in, touch the pictures, turn the pages and use eye contact
- put the book away when the child is bored.

Voice tips

- breathe deeply but naturally so you have plenty of puff for longer sentences
- don't let your throat muscles go tense
- clearly pronounce all the sounds.

Remember three things and you will hold your child's attention:

- draw on your **ENERGY**
- apply **VARIETY**
- make use of **PAUSES**...

...in other words, **get involved with the story.**

Tips on using children's books

It is a good idea to try and read through a book on your own before you read it out loud. Then you'll be ready to make voice and rhythm changes because you'll know what's coming.

The way children's books are designed is a great help to the reader. The spacing and the different letters all help you to change your voice and take a breath.

- Make voice changes where the words are put in (speech bubbles) or between "quote marks", or where the shapes of the letters change: loud when they go bigger and **bolder**; scary when they go spiky
- Take a breath when you see a full stop . or a question mark ? or exclamation mark !
- Use the line breaks to help with a sense of rhythm.

How to use this booklet

We've chosen examples from popular books and added suggestions from the Voice Coach on ways to read them. These should help you think about changing your voice and using your face and body.

All the extracts are marked to help you with the rhythm and tone:

- A | marks where you should pause, sometimes for a breath, sometimes to add to the atmosphere. A pause is a good place to be quiet for a moment - how long that moment is depends on the mood of the story and your listener. It can add to the suspense, it can give you time to think about what has happened, or what is going to happen. It can also give you time to change your voice!
- Where words, or part of words, are **bold** then stress, or emphasise, them. This will help with the beat and rhythm.

Although this booklet will not replace reading a 'real' book with your child you could have fun doing some of the exercises with them.

Making noises

Many children's stories are full of larger-than-life characters and crazy situations and your voice can show this. A lot of words **are** the sound written down and you can almost feel the word if you say it with enough energy.

Animals feature a lot, so have a go at pretending to be one:

bear	speak with a lot of breath in a deep voice
bird	say *'tweet-tweet'* or whistle up and down a few notes
cow	hum on lips, release lips into *'ooo'* sound, which makes a *'mooo'* word
dogs	for little dogs do a high pitched *'yap yap'*, for big dogs growl, then bark with rapid jaw movements
elephant	long, low to high, trumpeting sound through your nose and make an upward movement with your arm
monkey	open your mouth wide, show your teeth and on a breath repeat *'ah ah ah ah, ooh ooh ooh ooh'*
mouse	squeak in a high pitch
owl	thrust out your lips and use a lot of breath to expel an *'oooo'* sound repeating in short bursts
pig	breathe in through your nose in quick intervals to produce a snorting sound

Now try some **thing** noises:

bite	snap your teeth together
flying	high pitched humming sound, swooping up and down
man drilling	make a trilling noise with your tongue
ghost noises	make *'ooow'* sound, pout lips and send sound up and down
keep quiet	send breath through teeth to make *'sssh'* sound with finger at lips

Try out some noises in this piece from **Giraffes Can't Dance** by **Giles Andrede** and **Guy Parker-Rees**. The story-poem is written in an easy-to-read rhythm of 2 beats per line, easily felt if you tap on your knee. Use this to help give energy and variety to your reading.

Giraffes Can't Dance

VOICE COACH

*Ger*ald was a ***tall*** giraffe
Whose *ne*ck was long and ***sli*m** ▌

> first find your storyteller's voice. Keep it simple because that will probably be the one you use most.

He was *ve*ry good at ***stan*ding** still
And ***mun*ching** shoots off ***trees*,** ▌

> stretch your neck and do a munching sound

But ***wh*en** he tried to *r*un around
He ***bu*ckled** at the ***knees*.** ▌

*Ger*ald swallowed ***bra*vely**
As he ***walk*ed** towards the ***flo*or,** ▌

> gulp and swallow

But the ***lions*** saw him ***co*ming**
And they ***soon*** began to ***roar*.** ▌

> begin with a grumbling noise then explode the air out, open your mouth wide for the roar. Get your listener roaring!

"***Hey*** look at clumsy *Ger*ald"
The *an*imals all ***laugh*ed,** ▌

> try a roaring laugh

"Gir*aff*es can't ***dance*,** you silly fool,
Oh *Ger*ald don't be ***daft!*"** ▌

> to talk like a lion go for a deep, chesty voice since they are a big animal with a commanding presence

*Ger*ald simply ***froze*** up,
He was ***root*ed** to the ***spot*.** ▌

"They're ***right*,**" he thought, "I'm ***use*less,**
Oh I ***feel*** like such a ***clot*.**" ▌

> think of a giraffe's veeeeery long neck topped with a big, sad face - so pull a long sad face and, with a moan, you'll be poor Gerald

Try out some more noises with this extract from **It's So Unfair!** by **Pat Thomson** and **Jonathan Allen**

It's So Unfair	VOICE COACH
BANG went the door and	explode the B sound and extend the A - 'BAAAANG'. Say 'aaand' long and slow for suspense
SWISH went the broom.	say a long 'SWWWIIIIISHHHHH'
The farmyard animals heard Mrs Prout say, "***OUT, CAT, OUT!***"	when words are all in capital letters then say them loudly or, as in this case, crossly
"Meeow," said Cat, "that's so unfair."	for a cat say 'meeooowww' in a long, drawn out way, in a higher pitch than your storyteller's voice
Cat came round the corner, her tail in the air. "What happened?" asked the hens. "Are you OK, Cat?"	for chickens make an 'orrr' sound through your nose, slap your tongue on the top of your mouth saying 'tuc tuc'

Rabbit's Nap by **Julia Donaldson** and **Axel Scheffler** is a lift the flap book, so you would take your time looking under the flaps.

Rabbit's Nap

VOICE COACH

Where can Rabbit have her nap? ▌
The window seat looks nice. ▌
Bang! Clash! Who's that? ▌
Oh no! A band of mice. ▌

> yell the last two lines, or at least say them more loudly!

Children love beating out the strong rhythms and acting out the actions in **Bumpus Jumpus Dinosaurumpus!** by **Tony Mitton** and **Guy Parker-Rees**. In this short extract really go for the words in bold:

Bumpus Jumpus Dinosaurumpus!

VOICE COACH

There's a *quake* and a *quiver* and a
*rumb*ling around. ▌
It *ma*kes you *shiver*.
It's a *thun*dery sou*nd*. ▌
*Shake, shake, shud*der... ▌ near the
*slud*gy old *swa*mp. ▌
The *din*osaurs are *com*ing. ▌
Get *ready* to *romp*.

> try a big dinosaur roar
> *'graaaaarrrrr'*

9

Doing voices

The Big Concrete Lorry by **Shirley Hughes** is a story with lots of chat. Try changing your voice for the different characters which will keep up the pace. This is one of those stories it can help to read to yourself first, if you have time!

The Big Concrete Lorry

VOICE COACH

Out jumped jolly Joe Best. |
"Load of concrete you ordered!" |
he called cheerfully. |

> for Joe use a big, jolly, cheerful voice

"Not this morning, surely?" said Mum.
"I'm sure we didn't... " |

> for Mum add some panic to your voice

But it was too late. | Jimmy had already pulled a lever and the big drum poured out a load of concrete, | all in a rush.
Slop! Slurp! Dollop! Splosh!

> as you say these words, see the concrete flowing out of the truck...

Just like that! | It landed in a shivering heap right outside the Pattersons' front door. |
"Quick!" cried Dad, picking up a shovel. |
"Quick!" shrieked Mum, searching for a spade. |

> Dad's voice will be frantic and higher than normal

"Grab those buckets!"
"Fetch the wheelbarrow!" "Run for the neighbours!" |

> Mum's voice is now giving orders

"The quick-setting concrete is soon going to set!" |
Never had the Pattersons moved so fast. |

In this bit from **The Football Machine** by **David Bedford** and **Keith Brumpton** you need to sound like a game commentator.

The Football Machine

VOICE COACH

Mark 1 pounced on the ball. He dodged left. He dodged right. Then he ran straight towards the Ham goal. I Four Ham defenders closed in Harvey waited for the crunching tackle but zzooomm! I Mark 1 shot forward like a rocket. I The Ham goalie watched him nervously. I Skid – swivel – shoot – **GOAL!!**

> speed up your reading, starting low and building up...

> ...to a big yell at the end

Think about how the two gods, Rama and Hanuman, would sound compared to the two humans, Jaya and her mother, in **Rama's Return** by **Lisa Bruce** and **Katja Bandlow**.

Rama's Return

VOICE COACH

Rama ran through the forest looking for Sita until he saw the giant monkey-god. I "Hanuman," I called Rama, I "have **you** seen Sita?" I "No, I **haven't**, but **look**, it's raining **diamonds** today!" I

"Those are Sita's rings," I said Rama, looking up to the sky. I "She **must** have flown this way." I "**I** will help you to find Sita," I said the monkey-god. I

"I **like** Hanuman," I smiled Jaya. I "He was a good friend to Rama," I said her mother. I

> give Rama a firm, precise voice. When calling from a distance lift the voice slightly

> Hanuman could have a deep, booming, commanding voice speak from your boots!

> Jaya, as the daughter, needs the lightest voice

Thomas the Tank Engine stories by **Rev. W. Awdry** are full of speaking machines. How would an engine talk as it released steam, hooted and chugged its way along the tracks?

Thomas the Tank Engine

At last Thomas started. |

"Oh, dear! | Oh, dear!" he yawned. |

"Come on," | said the coaches, |

> try sighing in the pauses between the repeated words

"Hurry up." | Thomas gave them a rude *bump*, and started for the

> coaches might speak in a flat voice

station. | "***Don't*** stop dawdling, ***don't*** stop dawdling," he grumbled. |

"Where have you ***been***? Where have you ***been***?" asked the coaches crossly. |

> the repetition makes you feel as though you are chugging along the lines and helps you change your rhythm, slower, faster...

Thomas fussed into the station where Gordon was waiting. |

"Poop, poop, poop. ***Hurry up***, you," | said Gordon crossly. |

> give Gordon a deep voice

"Peep, pip, peep. Hurry *yourself*," | said Cheeky Thomas. |

> give Thomas a young, cheeky voice

"Yes," | said Gordon, | "I will." |

In **Anansi and the Magic Stick** by **Eric A. Kimmel** and **Janet Stevens** can you make a lazy and mean Hyena sound like a magician?

Anansi and the Magic Stick

VOICE COACH

Hyena woke up. | He noticed a pile of dust on the path. | He spoke to a stick leaning against a post: |
"*Ho*cus–*po*cus, *Magic Stick*.
Sweep this *dust* up.
Quick, quick, quick!"
As Anansi watched, | the magic stick swept away the dust.

> try giving him a snappy voice, speaking through your nose

My Name is Mr Fox by **Shen Roddie** and **Henning Lohlein** is full of very silly hens which gives plenty of scope for lots of clucking before, and after, you speak their lines.

My Name is Mr Fox

VOICE COACH

"But what an *AMAZING* actor! |
My name is Mr Fox *indeed!*" | the
hens said, | as they laughed, |
cluckitty-ha-ha, | all the way back
to the ball.

> at every pause make the chicken sound *'oooor tuc tuc tuc'* and use that sound where the book has *'cluckitty-ha-ha'*, getting your listener to join in

Showing feelings

Despair

Towards the end of the story in **Pingu the Chef**, by **Sibylle Von Flue** and **BBC Children's Books**, everything gets very urgent so really emphasise the words in bold.

Pingu the Chef

Suddenly the crate began to **shudder** and **shake** and then with a huge **bang** it burst open. | **Out** came all the popcorn! | **"Oh no!"** groaned the organ-grinder, | **banging** his fists on the table. | "I can't **face** any more!" |

Back at home Pingu and Pinga were gobbling up the rest of the popcorn as fast as they could. | They **had to** get rid of it before Mum and Dad came home.

VOICE COACH

use a voice that says *'everything has gone wrong'*

now make everything sound urgent

Love

This nursery rhyme is a gentle lullaby, perfect for practising your sing-song voice.

Bye Baby Bunting

Bye Baby Bunting |
Daddy's gone a-hunting |
He's gone to fetch a rabbit skin |
To wrap poor Baby Bunting in.

VOICE COACH

time for a cuddle, or is there a favourite soft toy to swing in your arms?

There is a bit of teasing going on in this extract from **Guess How Much I Love You** by **Sam McBratney** and **Anita Jeram**.

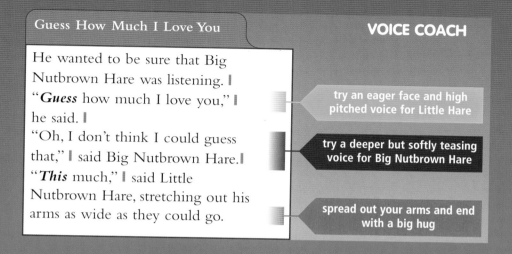

Guess How Much I Love You

VOICE COACH

He wanted to be sure that Big Nutbrown Hare was listening. |
"*Guess* how much I love you," | he said. |
"Oh, I don't think I could guess that," | said Big Nutbrown Hare. |
"*This* much," | said Little Nutbrown Hare, stretching out his arms as wide as they could go.

try an eager face and high pitched voice for Little Hare

try a deeper but softly teasing voice for Big Nutbrown Hare

spread out your arms and end with a big hug

Happy

What Makes Me Happy by **Catherine and Laurence Anholt** is full of short phrases that express different emotions. Take your time with each phrase and encourage your child to act out the picture. Here are some happy ones:

What Makes Me Happy

VOICE COACH

*sin*ging a *so*ng |

half sing it

*sk*ipping al*ong* |

use a light and bouncy voice

windy weather |

pretend you are out in the windy weather by speaking loudly

*fin*ding a *fe*ather and... |

*tic*kly toes |

say it with a giggle

a *big* | *red* | nose

touch a nose as you say it

Make the most of all the cheerful happenings in...

Hey Diddle Diddle

VOICE COACH

Hey diddle, diddle
The cat and the fiddle |
The cow **jumped** over the moon. |
The little dog **laughed** to see
such **fun** |
And the **dish** ran away with
the **spoon**.

> how high can your hands jump?

> **fit in a laugh, without sounding sinister!**

> **run your fingers around a nearby surface**

Sad

The animals in **Frog and the Birdsong** by **Max Velthuijs** come across a new idea.

Frog and the Birdsong

VOICE COACH

Hare knelt beside the bird and said, |
"He's dead." | "Dead," | said Frog. |
"What's that?" | Hare pointed up at
the blue sky. | "Everything dies," | he
said. | "Even **us?**" | asked Frog. |
Hare wasn't sure. | "Perhaps, | when
we're old," | he said.

> **keep Hare's voice slow and steady and low**

> **make a 'gulp' sound at the back of your throat before and after each time Frog speaks**

These are some sad things from **What Makes Me Happy** by **Catherine and Laurence Anholt**:

What Makes Me Happy

VOICE COACH

Rain, rain, **every** day.
No one wants to let me play. |
Someone **special**'s far **away**.

> **think 'it's not fair' as you read these and it should come out in your voice**

Can you feel sad for Humpty Dumpty?

Humpty Dumpty

VOICE COACH

Humpty Dumpty sat on a wall. |
Humpty Dumpty had a *great* fall |
All the king's horses and *all* the
king's men |
Couldn't put Humpty
together again.

use a soft toy on your lap to take the part of Humpty and bounce it off your knee

make your face really sad, pull down the sides of your mouth

Hunger

There is nothing hungrier than **The Very Hungry Caterpillar** by **Eric Carle**. He finally has a great big feast:

The Very Hungry Caterpillar

VOICE COACH

On Friday he ate through *five*
oranges, | but he was still hungry. |
On Saturday he ate through *one* piece
of chocolate cake, | *one* ice-cream
cone, | *one* pickle, | *one* slice of Swiss
cheese, | *one* slice of salami, |
one lollipop, *one* piece of cherry pie,
one sausage, *one* cupcake, and *one* slice
of watermelon. |
That night he had stomachache!

the fun in this comes from emphasising the *'five'* and then the *'ones'*, with a brief pause after each but building up speed

say this all in one breath

at the end, rub tummies and pretend you have a stomachache

Jack Spratt and his wife know how to avoid hunger.

Jack Spratt

VOICE COACH

Jack Spratt could eat *no* fat
His wife could eat *no* lean ▌
And so between the *both* of them
They *licked* the platter clean.

> show a happy tummy by
> rubbing it with satisfaction

Cross

More word pictures from **What Makes Me Happy** by
Catherine and Laurence Anholt.

What Makes Me Happy

VOICE COACH

Days when buttons won't go *straight* ▌
And I want to stay up *late* ▌
And I *hate* what's on my *plate* ▌
Why won't anybody *wait?*

> use an annoyed voice and
> emphasise the last word on
> each line

Being scary

To set up the scary atmosphere in **The Bump in the Night** by **Anne Rockwell** emphasise the marked words and skip quickly over the little ones.

The Bump in the Night

Long ago |

there was a *castle*. |

It was *old*. |

It was *cold*. |

It was *grey*. |

And it was | *haunted*. |

There was a *ghost*

in the castle. |

There was a *ghost* |

who went

BUMP in the night |

The ghost *howled* too. |

No one went in the castle. |

No one walked in |

its garden. |

No one picked

olives and oranges

from the trees

in its garden. |

It was a *haunted* castle.

VOICE COACH

notice how the effect would not be the same if it was written like this: *'Long ago there was a castle. It was old, cold, grey and haunted'*. **The little words give it rhythm**

emphasising the chosen words and speaking slowly keeps up the eerie atmosphere

do a ghost noise here by lengthening the *'owwowooooo'*

In **This Is The Bear and the Scary Night** by **Sarah Hayes** and **Helen Craig** lots of scary things might happen.

This is the Bear and the Scary Night

This is the bear alone in the park. |

"I'm not scared" |

These are the *eyes* which *glowed* in

the *dark*. ||

"WHOOOOOOOOOOOOO!"

This is the *owl* who *swooped* in the

night and *gave* the *bear* a terrible *fright*.

VOICE COACH

with a wide-eyed look and a frightened young voice try out *'I'm not scared'* 3 times, each time emphasising a different word and see how it changes the meaning - which do you prefer?

pout your lips and blow out shaking air

Max discovers a commanding voice and has a wonderful time in **Where The Wild Things Are** by **Maurice Sendak:**

Where The Wild Things Are

And when he came to the place where the wild things are | they *roared* their terrible roars | and *gnashed* their terrible teeth | and *rolled* their terrible eyes | and *showed* their terrible claws | till Max said *"BE STILL!"* | and tamed them with the magic trick of staring into all their yellow eyes without blinking once | and they were *frightened* | and called him | *the most wild thing of all* | and made him *king* of *all* wild things. *"And now,"* cried Max, *"let the wild rumpus start!"*

VOICE COACH

say the all the words to the next pause all in one breath

There is a lot of suspense in **We're Going on a Bear Hunt** by **Michael Rosen** and **Helen Oxenbury** as the family goes out - and back!

We're Going on a Bear Hunt

VOICE COACH

*Tip*toe!
*Tip*toe!
*Tip*toe!
WHAT'S THAT? |
One shiny *wet* nose!
Two big *furry* ears!
Two big *goggly* eyes! |
IT'S A BEAR!!! |
Quick! | **Back** through the cave! |
*Tip*toe! *Tip*toe! *Tip*toe! |
Back through the snowstorm! |
Hoooo wooooo! Hoooo wooooo! |
Back through the forest! | *St*umble
*tr*ip! *St*umble *tr*ip! *St*umble *tr*ip! |
Back through the mud! |
Squ*elch* squ*erch*! Squ*elch* squ*erch*! |
Back through the river! |
Spl*ash* spl*osh*! Spl*ash* spl*osh*! |
Back through the grass! |
*Sw*ishy *sw*ashy! *Sw*ishy *sw*ashy! |
Get to our front door. |
Open the door. |
Up the stairs. |
Oh *no!* |
We forgot to shut the door. |
Back downstairs.

| hold your breath in fear |
| build up a sense of danger with extra emphasis on the marks |
| gasp! |
| cry out |
| expel air through pouted lips |
| extend all the noise sounds |
| increase the panic |
| shout out the final instruction |

Naughty **Slinky Malinki** by **Lynley Dodd** scares himself into being good.

Slinky Malinki

Sl*in*ky Ma*lin*ki

was bl*ack*er than bl*ack*,

a st*alk*ing and l*urk*ing

ad*ven*turous *cat*. ▮

He had br*ight* yellow *eyes*,

a w*arb*ling *wail*

and a *kink* at the *end*

of his *ve*ry long *tail*. ▮

All over *town*,

from *bas*ket and *bowl*,

he *pilf*ered and *pill*aged,

he s*nitch*ed and he *stole*. ▮

*Slip*pers and *saus*ages,

*bisc*uits, *ball*oons,

*bru*shes and *ban*dages,

*pen*cils and sp*oo*ns. ▮

Then ...

VOICE COACH

speak with a slow, cat-like, stalking rhythm - the marked emphases will help you

get a bit faster but without rushing it

... after Slinky Malinki learned his lesson:

Slinki Malinki (continued)

*NE*VER again did he *ans*wer the *call*,
when *moon* shadows *dan*ced
over *gar*den and *wall*.
When *whis*pers of *wick*edness
*stir*red in his *head*,
he ad*jus*ted his *whisk*ers
and *stay*ed *home*
instead.

VOICE COACH

now slow down and pause
at the end of each line

wrap up the story with a
downward tone on the
final word

In conclusion

Thank you for going through this booklet; we hope you found it fun and helpful. Now you have discovered what you can do you need to put it into practice with **real** books!

All of the extracts we've chosen come from popular books that your local library will have, or can get hold of. They will also be available from bookshops.

If your child goes to playgroup, nursery or school, then get them to choose a book from there to bring home.

Getting hold of books does not need to cost anything – your **local library** is totally free and new books are coming in all the time. Many libraries also run reading activities and groups that might be suitable for your child – just ask the librarian, they are there to help.

If you do want to find out more about the power of reading, get hold of book lists, or find out about other activities then the best starting point is **The National Literacy Trust.** Call them on *020 7587 1842* or find them on the web at *www.literacytrust.org.uk* or contact them at: *National Literacy Trust, 68 South Lambeth Road, London SW8 1RL.*

Booktrust is an independent charity which runs the national book gifting programmes of Bookstart, Booktime and Booked Up which give free books and guidance to over 3.5 million children a year. Visit *www.booktrust.org.uk*

The extracts were taken from the following books

Title	Author/s	Publisher
Anansi and the Magic Stick	Eric A. Kimmel and Janet Stevens	Holiday House
Bumpus Jumpus Dinosaurumpus	Tony Mitton and Guy Parker-Rees	Orchard Books
Frog and the Birdsong	Max Velthuijs	Andersen Press
Giraffes Can't Dance	Giles Andrede and Guy Parker-Rees	Orchard Picture Books
Guess How Much I Love You	Sam McBratney and Anita Jeram	Walker Books
It's So Unfair!	Pat Thomson and Jonathan Allen	Andersen Press
My Name is Mr Fox	Shen Roddie and Henning Löhlein	Macmillan Children's Books
Pingu the Chef	Sibylle Von Flue & BBC Children's Books	Penguin Character Books
Rabbit's Nap	Julia Donaldson and Axel Scheffler	Macmillan Children's Books
Rama's Return	Lisa Bruce and Katja Bandlow	Red Fox
Slinky Malinki	Lynley Dodd	Puffin Books
The Big Concrete Lorry	Shirley Hughes	Walker Books
The Football Machine	David Bedford & Keith Brumpton	Little Hare
The Green Ship	Quentin Blake	Red Fox
The Very Hungry Caterpillar	Eric Carle	Puffin Books
This Is The Bear and the Scary Night	Sarah Hayes and Helen Craig	Walker Books
Thomas the Tank Engine	The Rev W Awdry	Egmont Books Ltd
We're Going on a Bear Hunt	Michael Rosen and Helen Oxenbury	Walker Books
What Makes Me Happy	Catherine and Laurence Anholt	Walker Books
Where The Wild Things Are	Maurice Sendak	Red Fox